A SHORT HISTORY OF BALLET

LE PAS DE QUATRE, 1845
From the lithograph by A. E. Chalon
Grisi   Taglioni   Grahn   Cerrito

A SHORT
HISTORY OF BALLET

By

CYRIL W. BEAUMONT

LONDON
C. W. BEAUMONT
75, Charing Cross Road, W.C.2.
1933

Made and Printed in Great Britain by Wyman & Sons, Ltd.,
London, Fakenham and Reading

To THE HON. GRANIA GUINNESS

In exchange for the daffodils

ILLUSTRATIONS

ILLUSTRATIONS

A SHORT HISTORY OF BALLET

THE precise origin of ballet cannot be stated with certainty, but it definitely derives from the several forms of composite entertainment variously styled mummings, masquerades, or interludes, which were of frequent occurrence during the 14th and 15th centuries. The mumming was given by persons disguised and masked who danced without mingling with the spectators ; sometimes the dancers appeared suddenly in the midst of an assembly, sometimes they made a more ceremonious entrance on foot or in an allegorical car, preceded by torch-bearers and musicians. The masquerade consisted of a number of gaily-decorated cars filled with actors in costume ; the procession filed past the personage it was desired to honour and, as each car stopped before him, the chief actor declaimed a laudatory poem or address. The interlude was a little scene of dancing, singing, and mechanical effects, given between the acts of a play or during a banquet.

An excellent example of the interlude, which for all practical purposes may be regarded as the prototype of ballet, was the splendid entertainment given in 1489 by Bergonzio di Botta, of Tortona, on the occasion of the marriage of Galeazzo, Duke of Milan, with Isabella of Aragon. It took the form of a great feast at which each dish was presented with an appropriate dance. This banquet-ballet, most ingeniously contrived and full of graceful allusion,

9

became famous throughout Europe, so that every petty Court aspired to give similar entertainments.

The new fashion found a warm patron in the person of Catherine de Medici (1519-1589), who introduced it to the Court of France, as a diversion for her sons, François II, Charles IX, and Henri III, while she retained a firm grasp of the government. One of the most important spectacles produced at her command was the *Ballet Comique de la Reine* (1581), which celebrated the betrothal of the Duc de Joyeuse and Marguerite de Lorraine. A full account was issued in a costly volume dated 1582, which, incidentally, is regarded as the first printed record of a ballet.

The author was a famous violinist, Baldasarino da Belgiojoso (later frenchified to Balthasar de Beaujoyeulx), who came to France in 1555. He was presented to the Queen who appointed him her *Valet de Chambre*, and later employed him in the capacity of unofficial organiser of Court festivals.

In his preface to the printed version of this ballet, Beaujoyeulx defines ballet as " a geometrical mixture of many persons dancing together to the harmony of several instruments." The designation " *ballet comique* " means " comedy-ballet," and the prime importance of Beaujoyeulx's contribution is that he succeeded in dramatising the ballet, for dancing, music, singing, declamation, and procession are dexterously combined for the expression of the theme, which was the tale of Circe. Some idea of the magnificence of this entertainment may be gained from the fact that it lasted from " ten o'clock in the evening until three and a half hours after midnight, nor did the length of it weary or displease the audience."

In 1588 appeared the first book devoted to the

SCENE FROM BALTAZARINI'S "BALLET COMIQUE DE LA REINE," 1581

The Frontispiece to the book of the ballet, published at Paris, 1582

practice of dancing, the *Orchésographie* of Thoinot Arbeau. This work describes in great detail the courtly dances then in vogue, the Pavane, Gaillarde, Volte, Courante, Allemande, Gavotte, Morisque, and nineteen forms of the Branle.

* * *

In England the ballet found expression in masques. Henry VIII (1509–1547) had his disguisings and revels, which became more elaborate during the reign of Elizabeth. But it was not until the accession of James I that the full influence of the *Ballet Comique* was seen, and the masque, with Ben Jonson, Campion, Samuel Daniel, and others as authors, Inigo Jones as designer of scenery and costumes, Alfonso Ferrabosco as composer, and Thomas Giles and Hieronimius Herne as *maîtres de ballet*, achieved full splendour. Among the entertainments given may be mentioned: *The Twelve Goddesses* (Daniel, 1604), *The Masque of Blackness* (Jonson, 1605), and *The Masque of Beauty* (Jonson, 1608). The masque disappeared towards the 17th century.

Thus ballet may be said to have originated in Italy, to have been developed in France to inspire the English masques, which in turn influenced the later French opera-ballets which were the foundation of modern classical ballet.

* * *

In France, during the reign of Henri IV (1589–1610), ballet became informal and less a poetic conception. The ballets consisted of *entrées* (entries) at different intervals of groups of masked persons in costume who, having executed their dance, made place for their successors. When all the groups had danced the whole of the dancers took part in a grand ballet. After this the dancers raised their masks and a ball began.

With the accession of Louis XIII (1610–1643) the ballets consisted likewise of a number of *entrées* having more or less relation to a somewhat vague theme. " Ballets," says a contemporary, " are plays in dumb-show, and should be divided into acts and scenes. Declamations divide the acts, and the dancers' *entrées* correspond to the number of the scenes." The number of acts in a ballet varied from two to five, while the usual number of *entrées* was thirty.

The *entrée* corresponds to what would now be termed a *divertissement*. For instance, the *Ballet de Madame Sœur de Roi* (1613) deals with the three regions of the air. In the first the *entrées* are Snow, Hail, Ice, Fog, and Dew ; in the second, Comet, Thunder, and Lightning ; in the third, Clouds, Shooting Star, and Rain. Again, in the *Ballet du Monde Renversé* (1625) there are eleven *entrées* : a gentleman walking behind his lackey, a fool teaching philosophy, a sick man prescribing for his doctor, a beggar giving alms to a rich man, and so forth.

But, whatever the nature of the ballet, and whether it was explained by words recited or sung, the sole purpose of the different *entrées* was to provide a suitable excuse for the entry of richly-dressed dancers in similar costumes, and wearing black or gold masks and diadems with plumes or tinselled aigrettes, who danced a number of figures generally containing some complimentary allusion. This particular set of dances was the recognised conclusion to every ballet and was known as the *Grand Ballet*. It was sometimes danced

"Les Fées de la Forêt de Saint-Germain," 1625. "Entrée des Esperlucates."
From a water-colour drawing in the Louvre

"La Douairière de Billebahaut," 1626. "Entrée du Heraut et des Tambours."
From a water-colour drawing in the Louvre

by ladies, sometimes by noblemen, but in the ballets in which the king elected to dance, a proceeding by no means rare, no woman of whatever rank took part.

The majority of the ballets given during the reign of the melancholy Louis XIII were characterised by a departure from good taste, and a marked tendency towards the fantastic and the grotesque, doubtless a natural reaction on the part of his courtiers. Two typical ballets of this period are *Les Fées de la Forêt de Saint-Germain* (1625) and *La Douairière de Billebahaut* (1626).

Under Louis XIV (1643–1715), the ballet became dignified and artistic. In 1651, while still a boy of thirteen, the king appeared in a ballet called *Cassandre*, devised by Benserade. This king made many appearances as a dancer, the last being in the ballet *Flore* (1669). Louis XIV, in accordance with his conception of kingship, represented exalted characters only, such as Apollo, Neptune, and Jupiter. Ballet made great progress during his reign due to his refined taste and the fact that he invited the collaboration of the best talents in his realm. Bocan, Beauchamps, and Pécourt in turn arranged his dances, Lulli composed the music, and Molière wrote many of the comedy-ballets. Berain designed many of the costumes and Vigarani was responsible for the stage effects. Louis XIV established the Académie Royale de Danse (1661) and the Académie Royale de Musique (1669). In 1672 a school of dancing was added to the latter, and this was the origin of the state ballet.

The ballet still continued to be a spectacle composed of dancing, music, and singing, but now it passed from restricted performance at Court to the public theatre. The themes were inspired by Greek and Roman mythology. Actually the ballets were operas

13

proceeded on horizontal lines, particular attention being paid to the pattern of the track described by the dancer during his movements. Already the development of ballet had given rise to a definite technique, for R. A. Feuillet, in his *Chorégraphie ou l'Art de De'crire la Danse* (1701), describes a number of steps.

Among the principal dancers of this reign were André Lorin, inventor of a system of dance notation; Pierre Beauchamps, who first laid down the five positions of the feet—he was also an excellent choregrapher and dancing-master to the king; Louis Pécourt (1655–1729), the best performer of his day ; Ballon (f. a.[1] 1695), noted for his lightness ; Blondi, and Lestang. Of *danseuses* there were Marie Subligny (1666–1736 ?) who succeeded Mlle. Lafontaine (1665?–1738), and Françoise Prévost (1680–1741), who succeeded Mlle. Subligny. The most favoured dances were the Bourrée, Courante, Chaconne, Gigue, Menuet, Sarabande, Passepied, and Passacaille. The Menuet, however, did not achieve full favour until the succeeding reign.

Under Louis XV (1715–1774), the epoch of Boucher, Watteau, and Fragonard, the grandiose manner of King Sun was replaced by a refined artificiality. The ballet grew still more elegant and many technical advances were made. In 1726 the *danseuse* Marie Camargo (1710–1770) made her *début*. She introduced the *entrechat quatre*[2] (1730), several types of *jeté*, and the *pas de basque*. To obtain the necessary freedom for the *entrechat* she adopted a heelless shoe and caused her dress to be shortened by

[1] F. a. = first appeared.

[2] It must be stated that some form of *entrechat* was known long before Camargo's time, but there are good grounds for believing that she was the first *danseuse* to execute it.

15

several inches, permitting the calf to be seen. This blow to tradition caused an immense scandal, but, since it permitted the execution of many new and pleasing steps, it was accepted. In 1750, another *danseuse*, Louise Lany (1733–1777), achieved the *entrechat six*. The same reign saw the execution of the *gargouillade* by Marie Lyonnois (f. a. 1746), a dancer noted for her ability to pirouette.

Early in the 18th century French dancers began to appear on stages abroad. In 1733, Marie Sallé (1707–1756), the rival of Camargo, unable to carry out at the Opera her desired reforms in the dancer's dress, crossed to London[1] and appeared at Covent Garden as Galatea in a ballet of her own composition entitled *Pygmalion*, produced on the 14th February, 1734. On this occasion, according to a contemporary report in the *Mercure de France*, she appeared " without pannier, skirt, or bodice, and with her hair down ; she did not wear a single ornament on her head. Apart from her corset and petticoat, she wore only a simple dress of muslin draped about her in the manner of a Greek statue." This novelty added still more to Sallé's graceful and expressive dancing, and created a furore.

In 1760 further pleas for reform were set forth in a remarkable work entitled *Lettres sur la Danse et les Ballets*, by Jean Georges Noverre (1727–1810), a choregrapher and pupil of Dupré, who, like Sallé, had to go abroad to secure recognition of his genius and opportunity to put his plans into practice. He produced ballets in most of the principal European capitals with considerable success.

[1] In actual fact, Sallé made her London *début* in 1725, and reappeared in 1730; but in neither case as a reformer of stage costume.

MLLE. LAFONTAINE
From the painting by Louis Boulanger

LOUIS PÉCOURT
From the engraving by Chereau after
Tournière

MARIE SALLÉ
From the painting by Louis Tocqué

JEAN GEORGES NOVERRE
From the engraving by Roger after Guerin

Noverre's *Letters*, considered as an exposition of the theories and laws governing ballet and dance representation, have no equal in the whole of the literature devoted to the art, and no book has exerted so incalculable an influence for good on the manner of production of ballets and dances. Noverre was not only a most talented choregrapher, but also a person possessed of an immense knowledge of his subject, and an unusual store of common sense and intelligence which he applied to the reform of every branch of his profession.

What were his ideals ? " To break hideous masks, to burn ridiculous perukes, to suppress clumsy panniers, to do away with still more inconvenient hip-pads, to substitute taste for routine, to indicate a dress more noble, more accurate, and more picturesque, to demand action and expression in dancing, to demonstrate the immense distance which lies between mechanical technique and the genius which places dancing beside the imitative arts." Those are his own words.

Noverre reformed stage costume, restored and developed the art of mime, decreed that all ballets must possess a good plot, and insisted that a dance must be designed not as a mere *divertissement*, but as a means of expressing or assisting the development of the theme.

He was the creator of the *ballet d'action* which had been foreshadowed in the experiment of the Duchesse de Maine, a ballet in which the theme was expressed entirely by means of dancing and mime, without the aid of a sung or spoken explanation. It was at Stuttgart, as *maître de ballet* to the Duke of Wurtemburg, that, in conjunction with the dancers Gaetano

Vestris and Dauberval, he first worked out his ideas. They were developed by Maximilien and Pierre Gardel, and Dauberval.

In 1766 Anne Heinel, a dancer at the Stuttgart Theatre, invented the *pirouette à la seconde*. The mask was abolished in 1773. This was the result of an incident during the presentation at the Paris Opera of Rameau's opera, *Castor et Pollux*, in 1772. The *rôle* of Apollo was taken by Gaetano Vestris, who appeared in the customary wig and mask. One night, however, he was unable to dance and the part was allotted to M. Gardel, who consented to appear provided that he was permitted to discard the wig and mask. The public were pleased and the mask disappeared. It is of interest to note that G. Vestris and M. Gardel are credited with the invention of the *rond de jambe*.

The costumes of the dancers of Louis XV differed to some extent from those of the previous reign. The men who executed the serious dance wore the plumed helmet and cuirass-shaped body as before, but the skirt was shorter, oval, of great width, and so hooped that it projected to a considerable distance beyond the hip. The dress of the *danseuses* consisted of the tight-fitting bodice and a hooped and panniered skirt, adorned with ruchings of various materials, generally lace or feathers. The perukes and costumes were in general more exaggerated than those of the previous reign ; on the other hand, the decoration of the costumes, in which allegory and symbolism played their accustomed parts, was more refined and subdued.

The principal dancers during the reign of Louis XV were Louis Dupré (1697–1774), renowned for the nobility and grace of his movements ; David Dumoulin ; Dupré's pupil, Gaetano Vestris (1729–

MYSTERY
*From the engraving by J. Le Pautre after
J. Berain*

DIANA
From the drawing by J. Berain

TRITON
From the drawing by J. Berain

FOLLY
*From the engraving by P. Le Pautre after
J. Berain*

COSTUMES FOR BALLET LOUIS XIV PERIOD

1808), a fine mime and unsurpassed for the expressiveness and elegance of his dancing; Jean Lany (1718–1786); Charles Le Picq; Dauberval (1742–1806); Maximilien Gardel (1741–1787); and Auguste Vestris (1760–1842), one of the greatest of male dancers, who held the post of *premier danseur* at the Opera for thirty-six years. The last-named was possessed of a sensitive ear for music, an excellent technique, a prodigious elevation, a particular ability to execute *entrechats* and *pirouettes*, and, what is rare indeed, he could adapt his movements and expression to suit any mood or style; lastly, there was never any sense of difficulty or stress in his dancing so that he seemed equally at home on the ground or in the air.

The chief *danseuses* were Marie Sallé (f. a. London, 1725, Paris, 1727); Marie Camargo (f. a. 1726), noted for the brilliancy of her execution; Marie Lyonnois; Marie Allard (1742–1802), celebrated both for her acting and for the charm and gaiety of her dancing; Anne Heinel (1753–1808); Marguerite Peslin (f. a. 1761); and Madeleine Guimard (1743–1816), famous for the precision of her dancing and for her piquant mime.

For the next fifteen years (1774–1789), that is, from the accession of Louis XVI to the outbreak of the French Revolution, there was a remarkable series of interesting ballets produced, for instance: *Médée et Jason* (1775), *Les Caprices de Galathée* (1776), *Les Horaces* (1776)—all by Noverre; *La Chercheuse d'Esprit* (M. Gardel, 1777); *La Fête Chinoise* (1778), *Les Petits Riens* (1778)—both by Noverre; *Ninette à la Cour* (M. Gardel, 1778); *Annette et Lubin* (1778), *La Toilette de Venus* (1779)—both by Noverre; *Mirza* (M. Gardel, 1779); *Medée* (Noverre, 1780);

La Rosière (1784), *Le Deserteur* (1784), *Le Premier Navigateur* (1785), and *Le Coq du Village* (1787)—all by M. Gardel.

Guimard dominates the scene throughout this epoch, her greatest successes being achieved in *La Chercheuse d'Esprit, Ninette à la Cour* and *Le Premier Navigateur*. Other dancers of the period were Auguste Vestris, Dauberval, and Pierre Gardel (1758–1840), brother of Maximilien. The principal *danseuses* were Mlles. Allard, Peslin, Miller (afterwards Mme. P. Gardel, 1770–1833), and Mlle. Théodore (afterwards Mme. Dauberval).

The advent of the French Revolution exerted a beneficent effect on stage costume. Dress was modelled upon the classic tunics and gowns of the ancient Greek and Roman republics. Fashion ordained that the materials must be light and in some degree transparent in order to reveal the beauty of the human form. With the adoption of the antique tunic it was possible to see the length of the dancer's leg, and now arose a real or fancied dislike to the exhibition of actual nudity on the stage. This led to the introduction of tights, which, while veiling the naked leg, would retain the illusion of flesh. Maillot, the costumier at the Opera at the beginning of the 19th century, is generally credited with the invention of the combined close-fitting knickers and long hose which still bear his name. It must be stated, however, that the use of tights was certainly known in the time of Guimard, who retired in 1790. The freeing of the legs enabled the dancers to leap upwards, sideways, and forwards, and turn in the air. Soon, the choreographic design included vertical lines.

M. Vestris in " Zaïs "

Mlle. Vestris in " Jephté "

Mlle. Lyonnois in " Les Fêtes de L'Hymen et de L'Amour "

Mlle. Vestris in " Acis et Galathée"

COSTUMES FOR BALLET, LOUIS XV PERIOD

At the end of the 18th century, France was superior in both dancers and choreographers, and their services were in demand at most of the principal European theatres, from London to Moscow. But the principal attraction of the ballets was still based on technical brilliancy. Noverre laid great stress on the importance of mime and expressiveness of dancing, but he was not so successful in translating his theories into practice. Dauberval, however, one of his best pupils, did much to carry out and develop his master's ideals. His most successful ballet was *La Fille Mal Gardée*. But the person who was to bring Noverre's dreams to full realisation was an Italian, Salvatore Viganò (1769–1821).

His parents were dancers and he was brought up in the same profession, special care being taken to develop his musical gifts. He studied dancing under Dauberval, from whom he imbibed the teaching of Noverre. Viganò married a Spanish dancer, Maria Medina, with whom he gave a series of successful tours from 1793 to 1803, at the same time producing occasional ballets.

In 1812 he established himself at Milan and, having been left a fortune by an admirer, he gave up dancing and devoted himself to choreography. In some ways he anticipated Fokine. For instance, when the *corps de ballet* took part in mimed scenes, it was the custom for the dancers to take the same pose simultaneously, or for the action to be spread over several groups, each expressing a different contribution to the general effect, with each member of a group taking the same pose. Viganò, however, gave each dancer a distinct individuality by allotting each one a different movement to execute, the actions being continually changed in accordance with the rhythm of the music and the demands of the theme. What Viganò attempted and eventually achieved was to express a theme by means of dancing and mime, both regulated in accordance with the rhythm of the music. The themes for his ballets reveal a remarkable imagination which at times rises to great heights. Indeed, the themes of most ballets seem childish and trivial in comparison with the conceptions of Viganò. He took the same care in the selection of the music for his works and, when he failed to find what he sought, composed the melody himself. His best ballets were *Promethée* (1813), *Psammi* (1817), *Dédale* (1818), *La Vestale* (1818), and *Les Titans* (1819).

An important contribution to the development of technique was the gradual appreciation of the increased facility of execution to be gained from being " well turned out." In all treatises upon dancing up to 1780, the feet are shown turned out at an angle of forty-five degrees. Camargo's brilliancy of execution was due to her being " well turned out," and Noverre in his *Letters* (Letter XIII), declares that " in order to dance well, nothing is so important as the turning out of the thigh. . . . A dancer with his limbs turned inwards is awkward and disagreeable. The contrary attitude gives ease and brilliancy, it invests steps, position, and attitudes with grace." But C. Blasis, in his *Traité Elémentaire ,Théorique et Pratique, de l'Art de la Danse* (Milan, 1820) makes " turning out " imperative to the dancer's success, and, in the drawings accompanying his text, the dancers are shown with their feet turned out at an angle of ninety degrees.

Carlo Blasis (1803–1878) might be termed the first pedagogue of the classical ballet. The son of a

AUGUSTE VESTRIS
In Les Amants Surpris, 1781

GAETANO VESTRIS
In Ninette à la Cour, 1781

MARIE CAMARGO
From the painting (circa 1730), by Nicolas Lancret

musician, he received a very complete education in the arts and studied dancing under Dauberval and P. Gardel.

In 1820 he set forth his theories on the technique of ballet in the *Traité* already mentioned. In that book he lays down a number of principles and establishes a code, the most important of which is the reiterated insistence on the value of line. The pupil is taught to appreciate this important quality by geometric figures which are afterwards expanded into delineations of the human body in dancing positions. In addition to many technical improvements, Blasis devised the position known as *attitude*, based on the statue of Mercury by Jean Bologne (1524–1608), and applied it to the *pirouette*, which he termed *pirouette en attitude*.

In 1837 Blasis became director of the Imperial Academy of Dancing and Pantomime at the Scala Theatre, Milan, and there he put his principles into practice with the most gratifying results. He formed a number of pupils destined to achieve fame, in particular one group whose success earned for them the name of *Les Pléiades*—Pasquale Borri, Marietta Baderna, Augusta Domenichettis, Flora Fabbri, Amalia Ferraris, Sofia Fuoco, and Carolina Granzini. In addition may be mentioned : Aminia Boschetti, Fanny Cerrito, Giovannina King, Carolina Pochini, and Carolina Rosati.

There were no easy paths to success at this academy. Pupils who entered it had to be not under eight or over twelve years of age, physically fit and prepared to remain for eight years, no salary being paid them during the first three years. The daily practice required of each pupil was three hours dancing and one hour mime. As the pupils made progress they were promoted to take part in the various ballets produced in the theatre.

As a choregrapher, Blasis composed upwards of seventy ballets and an immense number of *pas*. He is said to have been the first to make use of biblical themes as a basis for his dance compositions.

*　　*

*

To return to France, the French Revolution instituted a much-needed reform in costume, but disestablished the Académie Royal de Musique, founded by Louis XIV. Several attempts were made to utilise ballet as a medium for political propaganda, for instance P. Gardel's choric ballet to the strains of the Marseillaise (1792), and the later, more ambitious, ambulatory ballet, *La Fête à l'Etre Suprème* (1794). Gardel's most successful production was *Psyche* (1790), which was performed 921 times. The principal dancers during this period were Mmes. Gardel, Clotilde, and Perignon, Mlle. Chevigny, and A. Vestris, Milon, Goyon, Beaupré, Aumer, and Giraud.

Ballet revived a little under Napoleon, but the war between France and England deprived London of the French dancers. An interesting ballet produced during this period was P. Gardel's *La Dansomanie* (1800), in which the waltz was first danced at the Opera. After the Restoration (1815) the State Academy of Dancing was re-formed, and in 1821 English agents made a determined effort to cajole French talent to London. The negotiations were protracted but successful. The dancers, Lise Noblet and Albert, arrived. They were well received and created a renewed interest in ballet. Their appearance marks the beginning of the golden

SALVATORE VIGANO

CHARLES DIDELOT

CARLO BLASIS

JULES PERROT

age of ballet in England.   Soon, other famous dancers
visited London—Mlles. Bigottini, Brocard, Fanny
Bias, Mme. Montessu, and M. Paul.   The King's
Theatre, afterwards Her Majesty's, founded a per-
manent *corps de ballet,* and crowded houses were the
rule at this theatre, the Haymarket, and Covent
Garden.   Ballet began to outrival opera in popularity.

*   *

*

In 1822 an Italian dancer, Marie Taglioni (1803–
1884), made her *début* at Vienna in a ballet devised and
arranged by her father, F. Taglioni.   She appeared at
Paris in 1827, but met with an indifferent reception.
She continued to dance there and, on the 12th March,
1832, created the title-*rôle* in a new ballet called *La
Sylphide,* when she achieved a success which echoed
throughout Europe.   She came to London and
became the idol of the town.   Few dancers have
received a like remuneration for their services, for, at
one period in her career, Taglioni was paid the sum
of one hundred pounds for each performance.

La Sylphide was the first of the ballet's many
contributions to the Romantic Movement and marks
a new era in choregraphy.   As Gautier says : " After
La Sylphide, the Opera was given up to gnomes,
undines, salamanders, nixes, wilis, peris—to all that
strange and mysterious folk who lend themselves so
marvellously to the fantasies of the *maître de ballet.*"

Another point of interest concerning this ballet is
that the white muslin costume designed by Eugène
Lamy for Mlle. Taglioni—tight-fitting bodice leaving
the neck and shoulders bare, bell-shaped skirt reaching
midway between the knee and the ankle, pale pink

tights and satin shoes—became the accepted uniform for the dancer of the pure classical ballet.

Early in the 19th century, dancing *sur les pointes* made its appearance, although it is difficult to fix the precise date of its introduction. The shoes were not blocked, support being afforded by the darning of the toe. At this period *pointes* were generally used discriminately and with moderation to suggest the dancer gliding over water, or to convey the illusion of floating just above the ground, as though the dancer were an ethereal being unfettered by the laws of gravity.

Taglioni exercised a great influence upon ballet. She freed it from the lingering remnants of affectation, the artificial and stilted style of the 18th century. Her art invested ballet with a hitherto unknown quality of spirituality, emphasised by her technique, her prodigious elevation and ability to remain in the air at the highest point of ascent before descending, a rare gift possessed by two other dancers only—Auguste Vestris and Vaslav Nijinsky. She raised dancing almost to a religious rite. The ballets in which Taglioni achieved her principal successes were *La Sylphide* and *La Fille du Danube* (1836).

Among Taglioni's numerous male partners, mention must be made of Jules Perrot (born 1800), renowned for the grace and rhythm of his dancing, and for his excellent elevation, which earned for him such nicknames as "*l'aérien*" (the aerial) and "the male Taglioni." In addition to his ability as a dancer he was an excellent choreographer and produced a number of successful ballets in the principal European theatres. His best-known compositions were the celebrated *Pas de Quatre*, in which appeared Taglioni, Grisi,

TYPICAL COSTUMES FOR BALLET, EARLY XIXᵀᴴ CENTURY

Fig. 1. Danseur Serieux. Fig. 2. Danseur Demi-caractère. Fig. 3. Danseur Comique (Danseur de caractère

From Blasis (Carlo) "Traité Elémentaire Théorique et Pratique de l'Art de la Danse," Milan 1820.

Cerrito, and Grahn, and the *Pas des Déesses*, with Taglioni, Cerrito, and Grahn, staged in London in 1845 and 1848 respectively, and the ballets, *Esmeralda, Catherine, Faust,* and *Le Corsaire.*

Towards 1835 Taglioni had to contend with a serious rival in the person of Fanny Elssler, a Viennese dancer who was her exact opposite in that she represented the sensuous, highly-coloured side of Romanticism. The contrasting qualities of these two dancers have been summed up in the opinions of two contemporaries. " Mlle. Taglioni is a Christian dancer, Mlle. Fanny Elssler is a pagan dancer," asserts Gautier. " If Madame Taglioni flew, she [Elssler] flashed," observes Chorley. " The one floated on to the stage like a nymph; the other showered every sparkling fascination round her like a sorceress, with that abundance which finds enjoyment in its own exercise." Elssler made her greatest successes in *Le Diable Boiteux* (1836), *La Gypsy* (1839), *La Tarentule* (1839), and *Esmeralda.*

Other important dancers of the Romantic Ballet were Carlotta Grisi (1821–1899), noted for her interpretation of the name part of *Giselle* (1841), and for her creation of the principal *rôles* in *La Jolie Fille de Gand* (1842), *La Péri* (1843), and *Paquita* (1846); Lucile Grahn (1821–1907), whose best ballet was *Eoline* (1844); Fanny Cerrito, who made her chief successes in *Alma* (1842), *Ondine* (1843), and *Gemma* (1854); Amalia Ferraris, who is associated with *Les Elfes* (1856) and *Sacountala* (1858); and Carolina Rosati, best known for her dancing in *Marco Spada* (1857). Nine other favourites, although a little lower in the scale of popularity, were Theresa Elssler (Fanny's sister), Pauline Duvernay, Lise

Noblet, Mme. Alexis Dupont (Mlle. Noblet's sister), Louise Fitz-James, Pauline Leroux, Adèle and Sophie Dumilâtre, and Marie Plunkett.

However, by the middle of the century, ballet, so far as France and England were concerned, began to decline; partly because the singing of Jenny Lind focused public attention on opera, and partly because the art of ballet had become concentrated in the *virtuosi*, so that a ballet relied upon an individual dancer for its attraction and not upon the production as a whole. The exploitation of the *danseuse étoile* was also detrimental in that it caused the gradual disappearance of the male dancer who, formerly of equal, if not superior, importance to the *danseuse*, was reduced to the *rôle* of a living support. This led to male characters being taken by women dressed in men's clothes, a practice which carried ballet a stage farther on the downward path.

After Albert, Lise Noblet, Pauline Duvernay, and their contemporaries, the school of dancing attached to the Paris Opera produced few dancers of note, and in consequence became enfeebled, a condition aggravated by the fact that the extraordinary development of ballet in Russia—the new point of orientation—caused many of the best French choreographers to enter the service of the Imperial theatres. Taglioni, Grisi, and most of the great dancers of the second quarter of the 19th century received their training in Italian schools, and with a few exceptions, such as Emma Livry (1842–1863) and Léontine Beaugrand, the principal dancers at the Opera were mainly foreigners, for instance, Rita Sangalli, who created the principal *rôles* in *Sylvia* (1876) and *Namouna* (1882); Rosita Mauri, ever to be associated with *La*

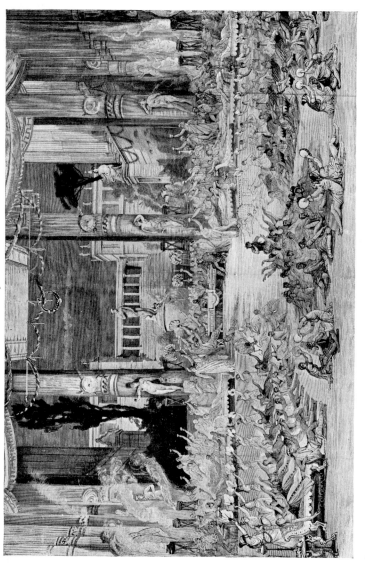

THE ORGY SCENE FROM "AMOR," AS PRESENTED AT THE SCALA THEATRE, MILAN, 1886
Choregraphy by Luigi Manzotti, costumes by Alfredo Edel
From the drawing by Lodovico Pogliaghi in L'Illustrazione Italiana

Korrigane (1890) ; Carlotta Zambelli ; and Aïda Boni, well remembered for her performance in *La Fête chez Thérèse*. In recent years native talent is again coming to the fore.

*   *
*

In England, from the 'fifties to the 'seventies, the ballet forsook the stages of the principal theatres and descended to the music-hall where it gradually expired. A revival took place in the late 'seventies as a result of the establishment of the Alhambra and Empire Theatres which, although dedicated to vaudeville, made a strong feature of ballet.

The principal dancers at the Alhambra during 1871 to 1914, in chronological order, were E. Pertoldi, Emma Palladino, Lucia Cormani, Pierrina Legnani, Emma Bessone, Maria la Bella, Mlle. Britta, Carlotta Mossetti, and Catherine Geltzer, and MM. de Vicenti and Tichomirov.[1] The choreographers were A. Bertrand, Carlo Coppi, and Alfredo Curti. The dance interest was concentrated in the principal dancers, the themes being primarily designed to afford opportunities for gorgeous pageantry and impressive stage effects.

The productions at the Empire were no less elaborate, but they were distinguished by a sense of restraint, largely due to the influence of C. Wilhelm, who wrote many of the themes and also devised the costumes for his ballets. Katti Lanner was responsible for much of the choreography. From 1884 to 1914 the principal dancers at the Empire, in chronological order, were E. Pertoldi, Kate Vaughan, Adelina Rossi, Mlle. Giuri, Adeline Genée, Francesca Zanfretta, Topsy

---

[1] The list does not pretend to be exhaustive.

Sinden, Phyllis Bedells (f. a. *The Belle of the Ball*, 30th Sept., 1905), and Lydia Kyasht (f. a. *Coppélia*, 17th Aug., 1908), and Enrico Cecchetti, Luigi Albertieri, Fred Farren, Alexander Volinin, Edward Espinosa, and Adolph Bolm.[1] Mme. Genée made her London *début* in *Monte Cristo* on the 22nd November, 1897, and remained a popular favourite for several years. Among the most successful Empire ballets were *Rose d'Amour* (1888), *Versailles* (1892), *Round the Town* (1892), *La Danse* (1896), *Les Papillons* (1900), *Old China* (1900), *Cinderella* (1906), *Fête Galante* (1906), *The Débutante* (1906), *The Belle of the Ball* (1906), *The Dryad* (1908), *Round the World* (1909), and *Sylvia* (one act version, 1911).

*　　*

*

During this period Italy and Russia were the two capitals of ballet. The Academy of Dancing attached to the Scala produced many excellent dancers although, perhaps, inclined towards virtuosity, for instance, Pierrina Legnani, famous for her thirty-two *fouettés*, Virginia Zucchi, noted for her *pirouettes sur la pointe*, Wilhelmina Salvioni, and Claudia Cucchi. The ballets given at the Scala were largely spectacular, being processions and *tableaux* interrupted with dances. The principal choreographer of the last quarter of the century was Luigi Manzotti, the composer of *Sieba* (1879), *Excelsior* (1881), and *Amor* (1886).

The revival of ballet as an art was to come from Russia. A state school had been founded by the Empress Anne (1693–1740) as long ago as 1735. It was directed by a Frenchman called Landé or Landet. His work was carried on by C. L. Didelot (1767–

[1] The list does not pretend to be exhaustive.

[*Photo : Roosen, Paris*

SCENE FROM "LES SYLPHIDES", AS PRESENTED BY THE DIAGHILEV BALLET, 1909

Choreography by Michel Fokine, costumes and setting by Alexander Benois

1837), called to Russia in 1801. He was a good dancer and an excellent teacher, and formed many Russian *danseuses* such as E. I. Kolosova, M. N. Ikonina, M. Danilova, and A. I. Istomina. In addition, he was a choregrapher of high repute and produced more than twenty ballets at St. Petersburg alone. His best ballet was *Flore et Zéphyre* (Paris, 1796), in which Didelot, for the first time, made use of wires for the purpose of enabling dancers to simulate aerial flight.

Many of the best French choregraphers successively crossed to Russia—Louis Duport, Jules Perrot, Mazilier, and A. Saint-Léon. The principal Russian *danseuse* during the reign of Nicholas I (1825–1855) was E. I. Andreyanova (1809–1857).

Presently the successes of Taglioni, Grisi, and Cerrito set a new fashion. Many of the French professors modelled their training after the Italian school, and Italian *danseuses* were imported to fill the principal *rôles*.

There were three state academies of dancing, one at St. Petersburg, one at Moscow, and one at Warsaw. The schools were convent-like in their seclusion of the pupils who were boarded, educated, and taught to dance until fitted to appear at one of the Imperial theatres. The Russian schools were unique in that they devoted equal attention to the training of both male and female dancers. In their ballets the beauty and grace of the gentler sex were sharply contrasted with the strength and virility of the male dancer.

On the 24th May, 1847, a Frenchman, Marius Petipa, arrived at St. Petersburg to take up the post of *premier danseur*. Eleven years later he was appointed *maître de ballet*. His first choregraphic efforts were little remarked, but, in 1862, he achieved a furore by producing in six weeks the five-act ballet *La Fille du Pharaon*.

Petipa's contribution was an incessant and unswerving effort to develop technique. He demanded from his principals the highest executive ability, and insisted that the rising dancers training in the schools should be fitted to take their place. Therein lay the strength of the Russian ballet because, in most other ballet organisations, technique resided mainly in the *virtuosi*, the *corps de ballet* being a minor consideration employed as a background or set in motion to retain the attention of the audience while the principals were resting.

Petipa's ballets reflected the spirit of the period. Nearly all boasted five or six acts and consisted of elaborate dances, beautiful groupings, and long processions. In general, they concluded with an apotheosis. Technique had been brought to the last refinement and ballet appeared to have reached its zenith.

Petipa died in 1910. His work represents a catalogue of almost incredible labour. He controlled the ballet for the best part of fifty years, during which time he composed fifty-four new ballets, revived seventeen old ones, and supplied the dances for thirty-four operas. Among his best-known compositions were *Le Roi Candaules* (1869), *Don Quichotte* (1869), *La Bayadère* (1877), *La Belle au Bois Dormant* (1890), *Le Lac des Cygnes* (1890), and *Koniok Gorbunok* (1898). The principal dancers during his *régime* were Mlles. P. P. Lebedeva, A. I. Prikhunova, M. S. Petipa, A. D. Kosheva, M. N. Muravieva, N. K. Bogdanova, M. N. Madaeva, C. Cucchi, A. Grantzova, A. N. Kemmerer,

MARIUS PETIPA

MICHEL FOKINE

[Photo : Sasha

[Photo : Barodi, Milan

SERGE DIAGHILEV

CAV. ENRICO CECCHETTI

founded his *Ballet Russe*, intended to reveal to Europe the manifold possibilities of Russian dancers in a new choregraphic setting, he selected Fokine as his choregrapher, a post which, with one interval, he retained until 1914. In a short while the poetic and dramatic qualities of his productions, added to the exact harmony subsisting between the movements and the music, made him the leading choregrapher of the day. After leaving the Diaghilev Company he produced ballets at most of the principal European theatres. His best-known compositions are " *Le Cygne* " (1904), *Les Sylphides* and Polovtsian Dances from *Prince Igor* (both 1908), *Schéhérazade*, *L'Oiseau de Feu*, *Le Carnaval* (all 1910), *Le Spectre de la Rose* (1911), *Petrouchka*, *Thamar*, *Daphnis et Chloé* (all 1912), and *Le Coq d'Or* (1914).

The Diaghilev Company, which endured for twenty years (1909–1929), with its extraordinary gathering of dancers, composers, and painters, was one of the greatest influences on all phases of modern art, and, considered in the days of its prime, it is doubtful if it will ever be equalled for the artistry and technical efficiency of its dancers and ballets, or, indeed, in the high standard exacted in every department by its director. During the company's career, sixty-three ballets were given, three being revivals; and five choregraphers were responsible for the productions. Fokine has been dealt with already, the following is a list of the others with the names and dates of their best ballets : V. Nijinsky (*L'Après-Midi d'un Faune*, 1912, *Le Sacre de Printemps*, 1913), L. Massine (*Les Femmes du Bonne Humeur*, 1917, *Le Tricorne*, 1919, *La Boutique Fantasque*, 1919), B. Nijinska (*Les Biches*, 1924, *Le Train Bleu*, 1924) and G. Balanchin (*Le Triomphe de*

Neptune, 1926, *La Chatte,* 1927, *Le Fils Prodigue,* 1929).

The dancers principally associated with the company were G. Cecchetti, A. Danilova, N. de Valois, F. Dubrovska, S. Fedorova, V. Fokina, T. Karsavina, L. Lopokova, A. Markova, V. Nemchinova, B. Nijinska, A. Nikitina, M. Piltz, V. Savina, L. Schollar, L. Sokolova, L. Tchernicheva, and E. Will; and A. Bolm, E. Cecchetti, A. Dolin, M. Fokine, A. Gavrilov, S. Idzikovsky, N. Kremnev, S. Lifar, L. Massine, V. Nijinsky, S. Novak, T. Slavinsky, P. Vladimirov, A. Wilzak, L. Woizikovsky, and N. Zverev[1]. The limits of this essay do not permit more than the bare mention of these names, but it is imperative to make extended reference to three of them.

Enrico Cecchetti (1850–1928) exerted a considerable influence on the art of classical ballet. A fine dancer in his youth, in later years he was equally renowned as a mime and a teacher. While it is sufficient proof of his eminence to state that he played a considerable part in the forming of both Anna Pavlova and Vaslav Nijinsky, it may be said that there are very few dancers of international reputation who have appeared during the last thirty years who do not owe something or a great deal to his training. During his fifty years of active association with the stage he was professor of dancing to the Imperial Russian Ballet, at both St. Petersburg and Warsaw, and to the School of Dancing attached to the Scala, Milan, and, throughout most of the twenty years' career of the Diaghilev Ballet, he was responsible for the daily technical training of that company.

[1] I have omitted the names of A. Pavlova, O. Spessivtzeva, V. Trefilova, and so on, who were engaged for special seasons.

ANNA PAVLOVA IN "LE CYGNE"
From the statuette by Rosalès

Vaslav Nijinsky was the greatest male dancer of the first quarter of the present century, and it is doubtful if his abilities, considered as a whole, have been, or ever will be, surpassed. He was a quite exceptional dancer both in classical ballet and character, a fine mime, and a choregrapher of great promise. As a dancer his work was not of the robust type, but neither was it altogether effeminate. He appeared to be of a race apart, an impression heightened by his partiality for unusual *rôles*, which were either animal-like, mythological, or unreal. He was possessed of an unusual technical ability; his *ballon* and *élévation* were really extraordinary.

Thamar Karsavina, a former *prima ballerina* of the Imperial Ballet, St. Petersburg, was the principal dancer throughout the first and greatest period of the Diaghilev Company, and it was largely due to her perfect partnership with Nijinsky, and her appreciation of, and sympathy with, Fokine's ideals, that the early seasons were so successful. She is a poetic dancer in the tradition of the Romantic Ballet, also a fine mime.

Two other companies of particular importance were the Swedish Ballet and the Anna Pavlova Company.

The Swedish Ballet was a private venture founded by Rolf de Maré. It consisted of Swedish dancers who, having proved their merit abroad, were later to be used to develop the art of ballet in Sweden. Jean Borlin was the *premier danseur* and choregrapher. From the technical standpoint the dancers were not equal to those of the Diaghilev troupe; moreover, the national temperament invested the work of the Swedish dancers with a certain coldness and reserve which contrasted adversely with the liveliness of the

Russian dancers. Nevertheless, the majority of the productions were distinguished by a definite sense of style-atmosphere and sincerity of aim. The settings, too, were often of a high artistic standard. Some of the ballets were based on national folk-dances and folk-themes, some reflected modernist trends in art and music. The company visited most of the European capitals and lasted for some four years of considerable activity, the first performance being given on the 24th October, 1920, the last on the 4th December, 1925. The principal dancers were Jean Borlin (1893–1930), Jenny Hasselquist, Carina Ari, Jolanda Figoni, Margareta Johansson and Ebon Strandin. The most successful productions were *Nuit de Saint-Jean*, *El Greco*, and *Les Vierges Folles* (all 1920), *Boîte à Joujoux*, *L'Homme et son Désir*, *Les Mariés de la Tour Eiffel* (all 1921), *Skating-Rink* (1922), *Marchand d'Oiseaux*, *La Création du Monde* (both 1923), *Le Porcher* and *Rélâche* (both 1924).

The Anna Pavlova Company, founded in 1910 by Anna Pavlova (1882–1931), a *prima ballerina* of the Imperial Russian Ballet of St. Petersburg, consisted at first of eight dancers engaged from the Imperial theatres. In 1913 the troupe was considerably enlarged in accordance with a contract to tour America. From this date the personnel was composed mainly of British dancers. The repertory was continually enlarged and eventually attained to thirty-four ballets and thirty *divertissements*.

Although the company enjoyed a highly successful career, its attraction did not reside in the ballets presented, but in the dancing of Anna Pavlova herself, whose supreme artistry gained her admiring audiences wherever she elected to appear. She represented the

SCENE FROM 'FOYER DE DANSE," AS PRESENTED BY THE BALLET CLUB, 1932

Choregraphy by Frederick Ashton, costumes and setting by William Chappell

[By courtesy of Bertram Park

SCENE FROM "THE SCORPIONS OF YSIT," AS PRESENTED BY THE VIC-WELLS BALLET, 1932

Choreography by Ninette de Valois, costumes and setting by Sophie Fedorovich

tradition of the Imperial Russian Ballet at its best, and kept to old ballets or new ballets produced on familiar lines. In status the Taglioni of her epoch, it may be added that no other dancer before or since has exercised so beneficial and stimulating an influence upon the art of ballet in providing aspirants for dancing honours with an ideal model. That influence, too, was world-wide, for during her tours she visited forty-four countries. The company was maintained for twenty years and only ceased with her death, which was universally mourned.

Pavlova's dancing was distinguished by its grace, airiness, and absence of visible effort. It was sincere, refined, marked by a vivid sense of style-atmosphere, and a genuine and deeply-felt reverence for the poetry of movement. She was also an excellent mime.

The principal dancers associated with her company were Hilda Butsova, Michael Mordkin, Laurent Novikov, Alexander Volinin, and P. Vladimirov. The choreographer responsible for most of her ballets was Ivan Clustine, later assisted by M. Pianovsky. The best known ballets and *divertissements* were *Amarilla, Chopiniana,* " *Dance of the Hours,*" *Dionysius, The Fairy Doll,* " *Gavotte Pavlova,*" " *Syrian Dance,*" " *Valse Triste* " (all by Clustine), " *The Dying Swan*" (*Le Cygne*) " *Autumn Bacchanal* " (both by Fokine), *Russian Folk-Lore* (Novikov), *Autumn Leaves,* " *Californian Poppy,*" " *The Dragon-fly* " and " *Rondino* " (all by Pavlova).

*　　*

*

Despite the severe losses which ballet has sustained in recent years through the passing of so many of its outstanding personalities, that art is by no means in decline. In Russia to-day there are excellent dancers being formed, even if their training has to be interrupted with a proportion of daily work in the machine-shops. Many of the famous old productions are still being given, although the modern ballets, as might be expected, are largely propagandist, such as *The Red Poppy*. The Opera at Paris and the Scala at Milan have recently received the stimulating influence of the co-operation of Olga Spessivtzeva and Serge Lifar, and Leonid Massine respectively. The lately established *Ballets Russes de Monte Carlo*—directed by René Blum and W. de Basil—which consists of a nucleus of former members of the Diaghilev Company leavened with a number of young dancers of promise, offers considerable possibilities when it has for choreographers L. Massine and G. Balanchin. In America, the presence of Michel Fokine and Adolph Bolm has resulted in many interesting productions being given, to say nothing of the numerous dance-groups that have come into existence. In England, the annual visits of the Diaghilev and Pavlova troupes, and Maestro Cecchetti's five years residence in London, are bearing fruit. There are many young dancers of merit emerging from the schools and several choreographers in the making who are striving under difficult conditions to acquire a working knowledge of their arduous profession. Moreover, thanks to the existence of such organisations as *The Ballet Club*, directed by Marie Rambert, which has Frederick Ashton for its principal choreographer, and *The Vic-Wells Ballet*, of which Ninette de Valois is both director and resident choreographer, there are opportunities for work to be shown to audiences gradually learning to appreciate ballet for its own sake.